A SILENCE OPENS

A SILENCE OPENS

POEMS BY

Amy Clampitt

ALFRED A. KNOPF · NEW YORK

1994

THIS IS A BORZOI BOOK
PUBLISHED BY ALFRED A. KNOPF, INC.

Library of Congress Cataloging-in-Publication Data

Clampitt, Amy.
A silence opens : poems / by Amy Clampitt. — 1st ed.
     p.   cm.
   ISBN 0-679-42997-2
   ISBN 0-679-75022-3 (paperback)
   I. Title.
PS3553.L23S55   1994
811'.54—dc20   93-26889
                                                   CIP

Manufactured in the United States of America
First Edition

TO THE MEMORY OF
MARJORY BATES PRATT
1896–1992

O the great stars.
The rising and the going down. How still.
As though I were not. Am I part of it?
—RAINER MARIA RILKE

The Outer — from the Inner
Derives its Magnitude —
—EMILY DICKINSON

. . . *un antiguo silencio esperando ser oido.*
—CECILIA VICUÑA

CONTENTS

I

II

III

IV

I

SYRINX

Like the foghorn that's all lung,
the wind chime that's all percussion,
like the wind itself, that's merely air
in a terrible fret, without so much
as a finger to articulate
what ails it, the aeolian
syrinx, that reed
in the throat of a bird,
when it comes to the shaping of
what we call consonants, is
too imprecise for consensus
about what it even seems to
be saying: is it *o-ka-lee*
or *con-ka-ree*, is it really *jug jug*,
is it *cuckoo* for that matter?—
much less whether a bird's call
means anything in
particular, or at all.

Syntax comes last, there can be
no doubt of it: came last,
can be thought of (is
thought of by some) as a
higher form of expression:
is, in extremity, first to
be jettisoned: as the diva
onstage, all soaring
pectoral breathwork,
takes off, pure vowel
breaking free of the dry,

the merely fricative
husk of the particular, rises
past saying anything, any
more than the wind in
the trees, waves breaking,
or Homer's gibbering
Thespesiae iachē:

those last-chance vestiges
above the threshold, the all-
but dispossessed of breath.

DISCOVERY

for Katherine Jackson

The week the latest rocket went
up, a pod (if that's the word)
of manatees, come upriver
to Blue Spring where it's
always warm, could be seen
lolling, jacketed, elephantine,
on the weedy borderline
between drowsing and waking,
breathing and drowning.
As they came up for air,

one by one, they seemed numb,
torpid, quite incurious. No
imagining these sirenians
dangerously singing. Or
gazing up yearningly. (So much
for the Little Mermaid.) True,
the long-lashed little ones
might have been trademarked
Cute by the likes of Walt Disney.
His world's over that way,

suitably for a peninsula where
the cozy mythologies we've
swindled ourselves with, on
taking things easy, might even
come true: sun-kissed nakedness
on the beach, year-round, guilt-free
hibiscus and oranges, fountains
welling up through the limestone,

the rumor of Ponce de León, having
found the one he was looking for,

living at ease in, some say
Boca Raton, others Cádiz. A last
bedtime placebo? Still, we keep
looking up. That clear morning,
just warm enough for a liftoff,
the fabulous itself could be seen
unwieldily, jacket by jacket,
in the act of shedding, as
a snake does its husk, or
a celebrant his vestments:

the fiery, the arrowy tip of it,
of the actual going invisible,
trailing its vaporous, ribboning
frond as from a kelp bed,
the umbilical roar of it
stumbling behind, while up in
the belly of it, out of their
element, jacketed, lolling
and treading, the discoverers
soar, clumsy in space suits.

What are we anyhow, we warmth-
hungry, breast-seeking animals?
At Blue Spring, a day or so later,
one of the manatees, edging
toward discovery, nudged a canoe,
and from across the wet, warm,
dimly imaginable tightrope,
let itself be touched.

HISPANIOLA

Note how the bear
though armed and dangerous
caring not at all for
dignity, undaintily
snacks on fat white things
paws strawberry meadows
lunges swinging smeared
through blackberry canebrakes
maps a constellated
dream of bee trees
snoring galaxies
the primum mobile
twanging the gulfs
of slumber   beatific
on the tongue
the kiss of honey :
or so we imagine
a hulking innocence
child's-play bedfellow
to the sapient
omnivorous
prehensile
raptor   world-class
bully : the rumor
brought to Alexander
of, in India, a reed
that brought forth honey
sans the help of bees
began it   a topography
of monoculture

blackening the Indus
Tigris-Euphrates
westward-spreading
molasses stain
island plantations
off the coast of
Africa leapfrogging
the Atlantic
Hispaniola
Spanish Mexico
Peru   Paraguay
along the Amazon
the Portuguese
the Dutch   the British
Barbados Antigua Montserrat
Jamaica   huger and huger
deforestations
making way for
raising cane   to be
holed   planted   cut
crushed   boiled
fermented or
reduced to crystalline
appeasement of mammalian
cravings   slave ships
whip-wielding
overseers   world-class
indignity   the bubbling
hellhole of molasses pits
the bear's
(or if not his, whose?)
nightmare

PAUMANOK

The humped, half-subterranean
   potato barns, the tubers
like grown stones, wet meat
   from underground a bused-in,
moved-on proletariat once
   stooped for, where Paumanok's
outwash plain, debris of glaciers,
   frays to a fishtail,

now give place to grapevines,
   their tendency to ramble
and run on, to run to foliage
   curbed, pruned, trained
into another monoculture—row
   after profitable row
on acre after acre, whole landscapes
   strung like a zither

where juniper and honeysuckle,
   bayberry, Virginia creeper,
goldenrod and poison ivy would
   have rioted, the wetlands
glistening at the margin, the reed-
   bed plumes, the groundsel's
tideline windrows a patina of
   perpetual motion

washed by the prevailing airs,
    where driven human
diligence alone could, now or ever,
    undo the uninstructed
thicketing of what keeps happening
    for no human reason,
one comes upon this leeward, mowed
    and tended pocket,

last resting place of slaves, each
    grave marked by a boulder
hardly more than a potato's size,
    unnamed but as dependents of
Seth Tuthill and his wife Maria,
    who chose finally to lie here
    with their sometime chattels,
    and whose memory too is now
    worn down to stone.

MATOAKA

for the tercentenary of
the College of William and Mary

1

Place names, the names of streams—
the Rappahannock, the Roanoke, the Potomac,
and that commemoration of sometime
    majesty, the James,

its tributary the Chickahominy,
the Pamunkey and the Mattaponi, each
what a people called itself once, subsumed in
    a gazetteer, the names

half-overgrown by the long quasi-
anonymity that is history: beyond
the sunken garden, the crape-
    myrtle symmetries,

past the foundation-stone surnames
(Blair, Wythe, Ewell, Brafferton,
Crim Dell), the wooded hillsides,
    in a rippling pause,

the gathered lisp of watersheds,
describe a lake, place-named—
at random, a homage half-absent-
    minded, a penance even?—

Matoaka. A woman's name, though
not the one we know her by,
or imagine we do. To Captain
        John Smith, our own

Odysseus—bright, contentious, crafty,
forever on the move—she'd been
Pocahuntus, well formed but
        wanton, still a child.

Nausicaä, only younger? A king's
daughter as advocate: that was
the story we told once, from which
        we've since recoiled

(we being history) in favor of
the hidden, discreditable motive,
the flagrant fib. Who was she?
        Ask Paul De Man,

for instance. Ask Nietzsche, Freud
or Lévi-Strauss. Ask Parson
Weems, while you're about it.
        Ask any woman

what she thinks, or thought she did.
The stories we tell ourselves keep changing.
Bronze-immobilized, demure in
        deerskin, the heathen

princess turns to bric-a-brac. As
kings' names do. As words—the ritual
twiddle of a once-abrasive contour—
        have also done.

Begin again. Go back to Majesty,
the word personified, a woman:
the dazzlement, the hankering after
    gold, fame, danger,

the smell, the pomandered stink
of it, of her, ruffed, wigged, gemmed,
powdered, breathing, to be adored.
    Back to the courtier

knighted at Greenwich, given leave
to name the shore he claimed, the year
fifteen hundred eighty-four of (mark this)
    our redemption, Vir-

ginia. Such were the forms
and usages, now quaint, of royalty.
Behind them, silences. Silence at
    Roanoke, on the Outer

Banks, what little there ever was
to remember long overgrown: the dunes'
expanse, the largesse of it
    past the unsullied

line of breakers, overrun
with grapevines, sassafras,
the massive green of cedars;
    the white birds, startled,

flying up; an unclad, hospitable
people bringing dressed skins,
the shimmer of a glut of pearls.
    Named Virginia,

a place without detriment or
sleight of language. Households.
Marriages. A girl-child
    named Virginia.

Five years later, footprints.
Ruined walls. A half-carved word.
What happened? By whose fault?
    Silence at Werewo-

comoco, seat of Powhatan,
who—as Captain Smith, his match
in guile, did not forbear to say—
    had his own majesty.

Silence at Henrico, the lands upriver,
and at Varina, where John Rolfe
planted the golden weed that one day
    would amount to money—

Varina, where after many inner
wrestlings, after consultations,
mumblings and catechizings,
    he'd bring his bride,

not as Matoaka or, any longer,
Pocahuntus but, renamed in Christ,
Rebecca. What she called herself
    by then is not recorded.

2

Christian names, surnames, place names:
Brafferton, called after a manor-
house in Yorkshire, whose rents had been
    bequeathed by Robert Boyle,

a man of learning and great piety,
to bring the infidels of Virginia,
across the water, out of their
    dark and miserable

ignorance to true religion:
Brafferton, a monument
to words we, or some of us,
    once listened to

in fear and trembling: divinity,
hell fire, the Fiend, Redemption,
Eternal Judgment: Brafferton,
    monument at last to

policy, tergiversation and
neglect. What happened? Whose
fault was it few gave credence to
    the awesome news

of Love personified, Who, having
undergone the worst, might still
prove to outlast undoing? Awe,
    in all the stories

we tell ourselves, is finally
what's durable, no matter how
we mollify it, no matter how our
    pieties keep changing.

What happened in the mind of John
Smith's nonpareil, a pagan
without a peer, grown nubile,
    then the shining

jewel of imperial endeavor,
now the mere sullied pawn
of statecraft and testosterone,
    who dares imagine?

After what dazzlements, what
threats, what stirred, fearful
increment of passion, as Mistress
    Rolfe, she crossed

that threshold, who can guess?
Concerning what she thought, miasmas,
quagmires, white birds flying up,
    the Holy Ghost,

deter us. Who's the more lost?
She had, at any rate, her uses.
Newly installed as convert, nursing
    mother and great lady

up the river named for his
increasingly unseemly majesty,
see her embark, chief showpiece
    of colonial bravado.

Now records of a sort begin:
of presentations, masques, levees,
of portrait sittings, wearing
    wig, ruff, mantle

of brocaded velvet; no less,
for a season, than the rage
of foul, fashionable London
    with its spiteful

stares and whispers, its catarrhs,
its bruited rifts and ruinings,
the whole interminable,
    fatiguing catalog

of latest things, the gartered
glitterings, the breathing
propinquity of faces: through
    a pomandered fog

of rooms and posturings arises,
stunningly vivid still yet
dim with distance, a figure
    long gone from Jamestown,

an ocean's retching, heaving
vertigo removed, and more: from
girlhood's remembered grapevines,
    strawberries, sun-

warm mulberries, leapfrog,
cartwheels, the sound of streams,
of names, of languages: Pamunkey,
    Chickahominy . . .

She'd thought him dead. She'd never
been so tired. There in London
a silence opens: Captain Smith,
    repenting to have writ she

could speak English, is witness
of how she turned away—she who,
out of a distance grown by now
    intolerable, had seen

the world, so called: brought face
to face with majesty, with empire, by
that silence she took their measure.
    Amicably, then,

she acknowledged him, and Jamestown;
as for his countrymen (in what tone
and with what gesture?), they were a people
    that often lied.

Details are few. At Gravesend, readying
for the crossing, aged twenty-one,
she seemingly abruptly
    sickened and died.

3

The chancel of St. George's, Gravesend,
gave her Christian burial. That she
would have chosen this we are less certain,
    given our own

tergiversations, the worn-down
pieties we stumble over,
that trip us up—gnarled rootstocks
    of the once counted on,

knobbed, knotted stubs, newer-
than-kudzu cure-alls, defunct
cultures—silk and indigo,
    the golden weed

King James once railed against
(correctly, it latterly appears)
as noxious, till persuaded there was
    money to be made:

tobacco money, sometime mainstay
of a college given royal grant
and charter to propagate a faith
    the courtier Raleigh,

having staked a last flirtatious
toss, and lost it, in
the shadowy predatory tentshow
    we know as history,

declared for: from beyond this earth,
this grave, this dust (he wrote)
the Lord would raise him up. Such was
    his trust. Less certain,

ourselves, of anything except
the omniprevalence of error,
here on the claimed soil of (in
    the words of Drayton,

who never saw it) earth's
only paradise, to stroll
beyond the commemorated
        names of Brafferton,

Blair, Wythe, Ewell, past
Crim Dell, down to where
mere water, rippling, preserves
        the name of one—

her true, her secret name perhaps,
but that's surmise—the world has heard of,
of whom we know so little: to stroll thus
        is to move nearer,

in imagination, to the nub,
the pulse, the ember of what she was—
no stranger, finally, to the mystery
        of what we are.

BROUGHT FROM BEYOND

The magpie and the bowerbird, its odd
predilection unheard of by Marco Polo
when he came upon, high in Badakhshan,
    that blue stone's

embedded glint of pyrites, like the dance
of light on water, or of angels
(the surface tension of the Absolute)
    on nothing,

turned, by processes already ancient,
into pigment: ultramarine, brought from
beyond the water it's the seeming
    color of,

and of the berries, blooms and pebbles
finickingly garnishing an avian
shrine or bower with the rarest hue
    in nature,

whatever nature is: the magpie's eye for
glitter from the clenched fist of
the Mesozoic folding: the creek sands,
    the mine shaft,

the siftings and burnishings, the ingot,
the pagan artifact: to propagate
the faith, to find the metal, unearth it,
    hoard it up,

to, by the gilding of basilicas,
transmute it: O magpie, O bowerbird,
O Marco Polo and Coronado, where do
        these things, these

fabrications, come from—the holy places,
ark and altarpiece, the aureoles,
the seraphim—and underneath it all
        the howling?

THE UNDERWORLD OF DANTE:

Canto IX

Seeing me stand there green with fear, my guide,
returning, the more quickly bottled up
the look that told me he was newly worried.

He halted, listening; for through that murk,
that black air's vaporous density, the eye
could hardly venture. "Surely in the end

we must win out," he said. "If not . . ."
A pause. "Assurances were given. But so
much time, and still no sign of anyone!"

I heard too vividly how he dissembled,
overlaying what he had begun
to say with words that differed so,

I grew more fearful still—more than,
perhaps, his hesitation warranted,
inferring from it worse than what he'd meant.

"Does anyone," I asked him then, "go deep
as this, into this godforsaken hollow,
from that level where the sole penalty

is hope cut off?" "Rarely," he answered,
"does any of us from that first circle
follow the downward track we travel now—

though I myself once did so, conjured by
the witch Erichtho, whose power it was
to mingle shade with corpse again. My own

remains were not long nude of me before
she summoned me to pass within that wall
and fetch a shade from the abode of Judas—

a circle farther down and darker, more
remote from all that's good, than any other.
Oh, I know the way, you may be certain.

This marsh from which so huge a stench goes up
girdles the doleful metropolis.
Rage will confront us here before we enter."

What he said next I now forget, my sight
being drawn by then to what appeared
lit up by the infernal glare within

those towers: three hellish things that had
in form and attitude the look of women,
blood-smeared, greenly garlanded at waist

and temple by a clutch of water snakes,
wildly writhing, serpentine-haired,
viperish: such were the Furies.

He who well knew these minions from the household
of her who rules where groaning never ends,
named for me one by one the foul Erinyes:

"That is Megaera to the left; the one
who ravens on the right, Alecto; and
between the two, Tisiphone." He halted,

as each clawed or stuck with open palm
at her own person, shrieking so fiendishly
I shuddered, and moved closer to the poet.

"Call for Medusa: she'll turn him to rock,"
regarding us below, they howled as one.
"What Theseus tried here is not yet paid back."

"Turn round, and keep your eyes closed. Were
the Gorgon to appear, and you to look,
all chance of our return would be foregone."

These were the master's words, as his own hands,
not to rely on any act of mine,
closed in an outer band about my forehead.

You who are sound of understanding, note,
I say, what trove of doctrine is concealed
beneath the seeming strangeness of this passage.

There came now from about the turbid moat
an uproar such as caused its shores to rumble—
a fracas of confused alarm, as when

a holocaust of torrid gusts, igniting
without check, engulfs a wilderness,
whose snapped limbs' scorched and crackling litter,

pulverized, grown irresistible,
drives the animals and those who herd them,
gasping and terrified, alike before it.

Uncovering my eyes, my guide said, "Look
now across that antiquated scum,
to just where the fumes are deadliest."

As frogs, when the predatory snake
pursues them, vanish, plunging headlong
into the muck, and squat there, hiding,

ruined souls, more than a thousand of them,
I saw in flight from one who, moving dry
of foot above the Styx, passed swiftly over.

Repeatedly his left hand fanned away
the rank air from before him—the one
sign he gave at all of being vexed.

Well aware of where this being came from,
it was my guide I turned to now, and at
a sign from him, I offered mute obeisance.

Ah, how terrible in indignation
that one appeared! He held a little rod.
I saw the gate give way, without resistance.

I saw him stand there on the horrid threshold.
"O you despised and outcast ones," he cried,
"why do you harbor such excessive rage?

Why such recalcitrance toward that Will
whose purposes endure unmoved forever,
whom to resist adds to your suffering?

What use to butt against what is ordained?
Your watchdog Cerberus still bears those scars
about the neck that are the proof of this."

To the foul thoroughfare he now returned
without a word for us, but with the look
of one who's spurred on by a care beyond

what human thought could possibly encompass.
We moved our steps to pass within, secure
now the angelic words had been pronounced,

and entered without raising any outcry.
Then I, desiring eagerly to learn
the state of those confined in that grim fortress,

cast wondering eyes about me. What I saw
was a vast, open desert place, the haunt
of ire and the most dreadful torment.

As where, at Arles, the Rhone goes stagnant, or
in the low-lying precincts of Quarnaro,
past the Italian boundary at Pola,

the burial mounds that crowd those graveyards make,
on every side, a rough terrain: thus was
it here, but far more grievously:

among the mounds the soil was all afire,
so fervently, each tomb appeared to glare
hotter than any smelter's craft has need for.

Each lid was up, and from below it came
the groans of one within, whose misery,
thus heard, seemed hardly bearable.

"Master," I said then, "what people lie
casketed within those sepulchers,
lamenting without end the end they've come to?"

And he: "Here lie the greatest heretics
of every sect, with all their followers.
More of them than you would suppose are thus

interred, like next to like, in monuments
of varying degrees of burning." Turning
to the right, we passed between those torments
and the high walls that encircled them.

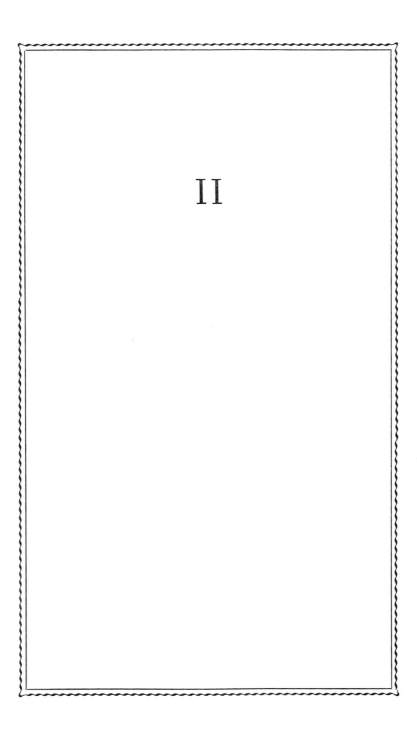

II

SHOREBIRD-WATCHING

To more than give names
to these random arrivals—
teeterings and dawdlings
of dunlin and turnstone,
black-bellied or golden
plover, all bound for

what may be construed as
a kind of avian Althing
out on the Thingstead,
the unroofed synagogue
of the tundra—is already
to have begun to go wrong.

What calculus, what
tuning, what unparsed
telemetry within the
retina, what overdrive
of hunger for the nightlong
daylight of the arctic,

are we voyeurs of? Our
bearings gone, we fumble
a welter of appearance,
of seasonal plumages
that go dim in winter:
these bright backs'

tweeded saffron, dark
underparts the relic
of what sibylline
descents, what harrowings?
Idiot savants, we've
brought into focus

such constellations,
such gamuts of
errantry, the very
terms we're condemned
to try to think in
turn into a trespass.

But Adam, drawn toward
that dark underside,
its mesmerizing
circumstantial thumbprint,
would already have
been aware of this.

WHITE

over the great inland
riverbeds   the greater
lakebeds   a runneled
skitter   by dusk a blur

swarms   interspersing glooms
of conifers the far
side of the pass with
mazily hexagonal

lopsided falling things
or substances   or stuffs
bear paw   ear flap   rabbit
scut   the mirror-haunch of

pronghorn   whiteness of whale
of glacial octopus
such thunderous accu-
mulations' drip and roar

snowmelt   sunbreaks   advances
and retreats   the polar
threatener   tossing to
cherry trees by parking

lots unseasonable
nosegays   leaving on wind-
shields these wet billets-doux
the snow is general

GREEN

These coastal bogs, before they settle
    down to the annual
business of being green, show an
    ambivalence, an overtone

halfway autumnal, half membranous
    sheen of birth: what is
that cresset shivering all by itself
    above the moss, the fallen duff—

a rowan? What is that gathering blush
    of russet the underbrush
admits to—shadblow, its foliage
    come of ungreen age?

The woods are full of this, the red
    of an anticipated
afterglow that's (as it were) begun
    in gore, green that no more than

briefly intervenes. More brief
    still is the whiff,
the rime, the dulcet powdering, just now,
    of bloom that for a week or two

will turn the sullen boglands airy—
    a look illusory
of orchards, but a reminder also
    and no less of falling snow.

Petals fall, leaves hang on all
      summer; chlorophyll,
growth, industry, are what they hang
      on for. The relinquishing

of doing things, of being occupied
      at all, comes hard:
the drifting, then the lying still.

THINKING RED

Swamp maples' unmasked sugars'
underhue, intense as madder,
alizarin or cochineal (a dyestuff

steamed from heaped corpses of an insect
native to Mexico: such the odd lore
of commerce in the exotic a bemused

E. Dickinson took note of): to
grub it out, the sense of it, down
to the madder's fraying final foothold,

the capillaries' threadily
untidy two-way form of discourse;
T. Hardy's ruddleman trundling

his dyeload of ocher; or
the bog-dwelling sanguinary
pitcher plant whose drowning dens

decoct a summer soup of insects
whose mainstay in turn is gore:
the clotted winter melancholy

of the sumac; hawthorn encrimsoned,
dogwood beaded the adorning
pigment of survival; the eyeball's globed,

dendritic riddle: to unencode
the hematite, the iron in the granite,
the carmine in the carapace, one has

to try to think in wavelengths. Light
has, we're told—I have it from G.
Wald—certain properties of waves

but also of particles. That's very
strange: G. Wald again.
Mind stuff, he tells us: physical

reality is mind stuff. In creatures
that puzzle over what it is, he says,
the universe begins to know itself.

Is this good news? I hope so. It's
that holdout, put-upon, reluctant
red (I think) that raises half a doubt.

NONDESCRIPT

There comes, in certain latitudes, a season
     no one would call the fall,
when the year-old foliage of live oaks,
green once but now a nondescript
dun or ocher, goes innumerably twiddling
     and twirling down

in the midst of a mist, a gold dust
     of pollen and petals no one,
so far as I know, has yet written of
as amounting to spring in the middle
of fall, or vice versa: the very notion
     of spring being mainly

defined, come to think of it, by the English,
     at least since Chaucer put it
in the month of April, ignoring all of this
in-betweenness, this process that's less
an advent than it is a wandering vaguely
     nel mezzo del cammin:

not to speak of an April brown down under, or
     a perennial tropical zone,
in Italy also not only the live oaks' nondescript but the camphor trees' untimely
crimson keeps on coming down, coming down
     in the midst of the green.

THE HORNED RAMPION

Daily, out of that unfamiliar,
entrancingly perpendicular
terrain, some new
and, on minute
inspection, marvelous
thing would be opening—

yet another savory-
flowery permutation
of selene or salvia,
of scabious, of rockrose,
of evening primrose, of
bellflower such as the one

I'd never before laid eyes
on the like of: spurred,
spirily airy, a sort of
stemborne baldachin,
a lone, poised,
hovering rarity, hued

midway between the clear
azure of the rosemary
and the aquilegia's
somberer purple,
that turned out to be
named the horned rampion.

Next day it was no longer
singular but several;
the day after, many.
Within a week it was
everywhere, had become
the mere horned rampion,

had grown so familiar
I forgot it, had not
thought of it since,
it seems, until the moment
a volume of the Encyclopedia
Britannica, pulled down

for some purpose, fell open
at random, and there was
the horned rampion, named
and depicted, astonishing
in memory as old love
reopened, still quivering.

BAYOU AFTERNOON

for Joy Scantlebury

Out of the imprecise, the murk
of bright and dark, the wavering
at the bayou's edge, such

specificity: the egret's samite,
filamented, barbed and folded,
hourly preened and realigned,

just so: the unmistakably,
topheavily crested and cravatted
kingfisher: just so, the wading

ungainly fantasy, paintbox-
tinged pink and green, that's
called the spoonbill, back from

a rim known as extinction: just
so, that afternoon, the colonies,
along the streambank, of lilies,

each perishable hieroglyph
filamented, in a flourish, with
a stroke of purple. Meanwhile,

out on the Gulf, the airs and
vapors had grown monumental,
their huge purple a flickering

testament to, at the rim we
necessarily inhabit, a happenstance
still brimming, still uncodified.

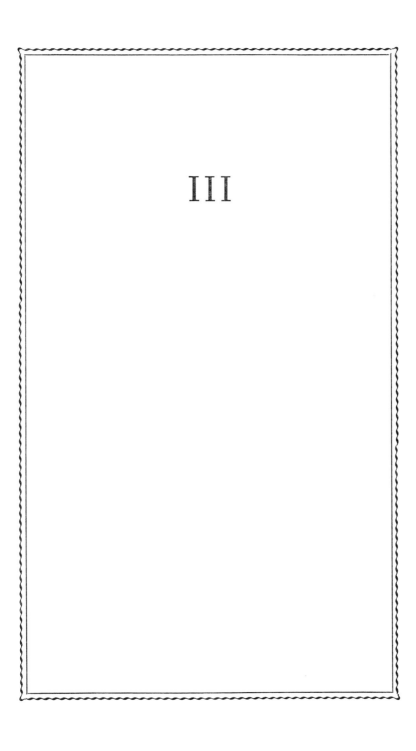

III

IN UMBRIA:
A SNAPSHOT

The coldest, wettest spring within living memory
is the way they describe it. At Assisi
there have been six straight weeks of rain.
They blame it on the Gulf War, of which Melina
happily, for the time being, knows nothing.
A vehement *"Goodness!"* is her fiercest expletive.

Little runaway, forget-me-not-eyed, ringlet-
aureoled refugee from a fresco by Lorenzetti—
all those gold-leaf rigors, the theological
murk underneath—whom nobody can begin to
keep up with, or anyhow nobody human. *Her*
peers are the brown-faced saint's familiars:

he of the caninely grinning lope, they of
the barnyard strut and chuckle, the noon-hour
flurry, by the recycled temple of Minerva, of
brakings and hoverings, structure and function
of wingbeats she'd been gleefully part of
minutes before going romping off into a dark

she knows nothing about—or is one, at a year
and eight months, already prey to nightmares?—
that goes back to before the Gulf War. *"La bimba!"*—
the reverberation accused us along the catacomb
she stood crying in, consoled by who knows, by now,
how many strangers: Kodachromed all over Umbria

beaming, the crowd scene in the café or the square
perceived as benediction, one unendingly
extended family: or come to a halt, as now,
halfway up an impossible hill, aware of being
small and alone: incipience a spinning globe
(look! the sun's out), all its great spaces opening.

BIRDHAM

Hemmed by loud seas,
by fractured granite, by island
treescapes each spined like a hedgehog,
as well as wild roses' formidable
coppices, on beholding
an up-late-in-daylight
porcupine, its thicketed
shambling perpendicular a stupor
of armament, I thought

of Birdham, all meek horizontals,
blurred margins, sea meeting land
among lanes and hedgerows:
of mild, tall, approachable
roses and delphiniums, a robin
scavenging the tablecloth at
teatime: of exclaiming, one evening,
"Barbara, there's a hedgehog
out in the garden!"

"Oh," my friend complacently
said then, "that's Henry."
Far-off, long-settled
Birdham is like that.

AT EASTERLY

Fog all day, skim
milk to gruel
and back without
a stirring, a
single needle-
leaf's displacement:
pine trees' idi-
osyncrasy
of layering
and stance, seen from
out there, no freak
but rather as
though graven and
ordained to be
so: expressive
of (it comes to
seem) some patience,
comprehending
instabilities
of wind and
tidefall, under-
writing the running-
through-the-fingers
expenditure
of moonlight on
water, lending
ballast against
vertigo as
tent-pole spruce boles
queasily, at

day's end, begin
to weave and sway:
containing the
far-out reef-slam
of a turmoil
whose rumor stirs,
in these joists and
rafters, tremors
boding of no
more than the least
pointillist tip-
toe expanding
to just such a
downpour as
Grattan Condon
(who's dead now, but
whose intent goes
on without him)
put the roof up
that we're under
to listen for.

HANDED DOWN

Raymond Hodgkins, his dragger last seen
in heavy seas off Schoodic, night falling
and still no word of him; and before him

Buddy Closson, Herb Damon, Ben Day,
Clyde Haskell, Larry Robbins senior,
Alan Thompson: the roll of the names

goes on and on, goes back thirty years
to Ray Dunbar, the day the *Lillian Mae*
broke up between the bar islands: back

to that scene, the men gathering, the women
waiting above the inlet, the skirts they still
wore in those days blowing out behind them

(a painterly embellishment handed down
by Grattan Condon) as one, unanimous
the way gulls are, heading into the wind.

Divers went searching, but found no body;
one of them tripped, fouled in a kelp bed,
came close to drowning. Days passed; nothing.

Then Vin Young—it was Vin, not Vic, his twin,
the way they remember—no more than thirteen,
but old enough to go out hauling, dreamed

one night, and woke up still afraid, of
finding Ray. He told only Vic, the two of them
dawdled and puttered until their father

said, "You kids better get out there
if you aim to earn your keep." So
they went out, and that day, sure enough

(the way they tell it), saw something floating,
a body, and it was Ray Dunbar. It's the names,
the roll call handed on and let down

in heavy seas, the visibility near zero,
the solitude total, night falling—it's the names
of the dead, kept alive, they still hold on to.

MANHATTAN

for Phoebe Hoss

GRACE CHURCH

A day of gusts and puddles, the vivid
litter of a season no better ordered
than the debris we carry with us, each,

of hurt and counter-hurt, attachments
wrenched from or slowly shed, engulfs
the maudlin fretwork, the pieced glass.

Like kids, unwilling, sent back to school,
we learn how our own history has its exits
and its entrances, its waning phase.

Once, even the wry sendoff to Reno
seemed expansive; the mists and gustings
of champagne, the shipboard trysts,

slip now into the backward and abysm
with the mortgage burnings, tinkling
martini pitchers on the beach at Gilgo;

Southold with its steamer clams, beer
and garrulity; the boozeless week at
Flynn's—Fire Island beach fires,

sunsets on Great South Bay; birthday
bashes, welcomes home, milestone
observances assembling yet again

the loose, patched, decades-frayed,
half-accidental, half-willed Old Crowd.
Habitual molecules have their gatherings

and dispersals: we learn how our,
how every history comes down to
this, the encounter with the starved

handclasp from the wheelchair: to share
the bed of this, seeing it distend,
begin to ooze like an edema: death,

that blear-eyed, feathery noise. He'd
kept a careful regimen—no alcohol,
a daily six-mile run—had coaxed

a rooftop lotus into bloom, thrown
memorable parties. An *Augenblick*
through tokay lampshade-glades,

trompe-l'oeil and calfskin: fey connoisseur
of the unlooked-for (the diagnosis:
cancer of the liver) sharing tête-à-tête

a glimpse he'd noted as he ran: in
Central Park, through early-morning
mist, a surreptitious crew of women,

unmistakably Chinese, with raised
poles harvesting the dun produce
of a stand of ginkgo trees. An

eyeblink of the hand-to-hand, the
elfin bubble of the incorporeal
settles, shivering, as the mind is stilled.

CHARLES STREET

Transplanted from the Carolinas, from
Pittsfield and Sewickley, the raw demes
of Appalachia and Iowa, from the arterio-

sclerotic clot across the Hudson, among
the walkups, the ginkgo-shaded side streets
of Greenwich Village, to claim the privilege

of ignoring one's next-door neighbors, of
getting drunk in bars, of being sick in
hallways, of fornications in strange beds,

solipsist terrors of the mad, the marginal,
the merely totally confused—we'd come
to listen for the West Side Highway's

nightlong silken seethe, for foghorns
mourning the tenor of the day before it
opened, for subliminal harmonic tremors

as the old *Queen Mary* cleared her larynx;
to spy out trivial marvels in mundane
bazaars: I think of the Fourteenth Street

refreshment stand whose reamers gushed,
one balefully faceless fall, with juices
not of crushed citrus or papaya, but

of crammed red-parchment pomegranates'
casefuls of rubies, each with its nucleus
of possibility encysted at the center,

translucent hemoglobin of exotic groves
adrift among dead-end chicaneries, bins
of cut-rate merchandise, all-weather

scavengers of trashcans, the misfit
solitaries, dislocated extended families
from Puerto Rico, the dwindling remnant

of the native Irish. From symbiotic
venoms of achieve or be undone, the candor
of whatever community distilled its own

scarce nostrum finds a remembered center
in gatherings, the back garden lantern-
strung, on Charles Street, where from

occasion to occasion a mazy entity affirmed
itself in loose sendoff talk of ashrams,
of reunions so exotic, the sheer prospect

so like a gem I'd wear it home
and watch it turn into the dawn, an opal's
packed circumference: nowhere to stash it

but in the scuffed insomniac luggage
of a future lately overpast. The scions
of a new uprooting gather now, or wake alone

and scared, on Charles Street; the ginkgos'
bare, bud-nubbed brooms purvey the wizened
gemstones of a dun, unasked-for fruit.

December, and again an exit, the slow
aftershock of months-old news (inoperable
cancer of the pancreas). At Grace Church

the day after the equinox, we'd seen him
wheeled in starving, the awful door
blown to. Today, a half-involuntary

particle in the shifting habitual
concourse that floods the gangway
as the slung barrier recedes, to board

the shunted, hooting, double-snub-
nosed tub he was as much at home in as
an owned house (he'd been a seaman,

had the lover of precision's ear
for discord; for him, unjaded by
familiarity, it was as though the harbor

could do no wrong), is to feel the stale
hour lose its nerve, grow listless, slip,
marked only, if at all, by some braced

gull's half-obliterated outcry, toward
the solstice: toward the annual foreboding of
a swerve, this year, through outer cold

no longer to be bridged. Hart Crane's
great cabled lyre corrodes: a frayed
strand one day broke, dangled, struck

and killed between the boroughs' apoplectic
upthrust and wrecking claw, the stunned
queue, the gusted, elbowing guffaws,

True Believers in the sanctity of Wear
and Tear, the quaint ordeal of Trickle-Down,
a continent, a people, a consensus unmoored

from any history at all—the whole mythic
mishegass that used him up. Asked why
he shrugged—he shrugged a lot, drank

still more, grew more and more low-
key—he would have murmured, "Is there
a better system, then?" The fossil carbon

of whatever outrage still smoldered in the
wreckage, that fall day, we turned away from.
Beside the stripped carapace of Ellis Island,

gowned Liberty in effigy lofts her
Promethean fable on the decades-sodden
pilings, bile and verdigris—crass icon

of the possible, the yet-, the never-to-be-
ventured-on. From the railing he'd drink in
this daily brew of hubris and sea air

as from a stein. The random particles
disbanding, the estuarial currents merge:
the mind gropes toward its own recessional.

THE WAR MEMORIAL

The rain-god Tlaloc, hungering for blood,
the war-god, hummingbird-gartered
Huitzilopochtli, the drugged booty

of a huger, cleverer hunger, stir
in a museum hall of nightmare, where
Asshur the bellicose and Marduk, who

rode forth to set the world in order,
are neighbors, where the drifts and dunes
of long-immobilized cuneiform begin

to move again, a bas-relief of dread
like the long scar, the black cicatrice
of memory not yet embalmed but raw,

those drifts of origami at its foot:
to trace whose length is to reopen
what George Fox, compelled at Lichfield

to take off his shoes, walked barefoot
in—the channel of the blood of those
who fell. For what? Can someone tell us?

'EIGHTY-NINE

in memory of Andrew Myers

Season of contaminated mists,
    of premises abandoned, the heartland
curdling in a spate of messages—
    the sequined smirk, the flicker
of apocalypse only the young, whose
    prospects who cares to imagine,
        can stand to dance to:
    season of scavengers: how is it,
in the evening light above the landfill
the gulls, massed, hovering, diaphanous,
    take on the look of angels?

John Keats at Winchester, fair-weather
    scavenger of what pleases the eye,
was for the nonce persuaded by just
    such appearances: the stubblefields
suffused, the season's lineaments
    discerned as halfway human. Time
        equivocates: though no epiphany
    outstays the wholly dividual rupture,
above the water meadows' jewelweed and
fennel the midge-swarm hangs, its scrim
    untorn, as without interruption.

Continuity of the winged, the windborne,
    the rooted: reassurance of the made,
the handed down, the durable: glyph
    and vesper bell, trodden cloister and
walled playing field: it was as though,
    that evening, the young athletes
        in their perfect whites, the bat's
    pock, the patter of applause—as though
pure sport had turned the key against
fever and shivering, nausea, hemorrhage,
    the entire obscenity of dying young.

O, or of dying at any age, by degrees
    or by accident: to be alive at all
is no more than an ambuscade, eluding
    the presence of angels, since it is
in the nature of angels to be terrible:
    thralled to the heavings of a visceral
        mass peepholed with ganglia,
    while somewhere in there the big-eyed rabbit
of delirium, cowering, scared witless, waits:
O dense as spiders' spinning trajectories
    at summer's end are these inklings

of undoing; or as the seasonal downpour
    distends to a cording of thongs and sinews,
a knout of wet one gives oneself up to,
    soaked through, having made one's peace with
whatever the elements can do. Or almost.
    For beyond that peace is the shape of
        calamity nobody is ever
    ready for: on a day at the end of summer,
a car going off the road, a mangling
incendiary gasp, and for four young athletes,
    without harbinger all is over.

He was twenty, the one I knew: T-shirted,
    dripping from the shower is the way
I remember him, just passing through. Such
    images console somehow. When the note came,
with the clipping, I saw the capacity for grief
    sit there, in the face of such cautery, inert
        with refusal. But the mother
    had already entered (as she'd later put it)
a place where the things people do for one
have no names: such an inrush, she lived floating
    in a deep lake of it, of that charity.

Mourning her own unborn, uncosseted
    grandchildren, she'd have gone over and over
the lack of evidence of design in the event,
    having met with the messengers, having
found them (and even the archangels are,
    after all, only messengers) inscrutable.
        O how intricate a patterning
    in the bracken's yellowing diminishment,
the hornet's fallen factories; in the squirrel's
uncalculated leap a smoke-ring wavelength's
    theorem still fluttering.

What, then, notwithstanding the evidence
    of dance at the heart of the matter,
whatever matter may be, of all the arson
    and concussion, of that blister they call
the Sea of Tranquillity? What of the atom,
    its core no dance hall but a regardless
        demos, disaster's hotbed?
    For all our jargon of knowing and managing,
for all our summoning of the forces of order,
in a season of sour rain, how happily
    we looked at anarchy in bloom.

Strange, what a year it was altogether
　　for anniversaries—all the might-have-
beens of human nature seemingly reborn;
　　of, even, that November weekend—
the all-night bus ride, the carried candles,
　　an exuberance of rage over being lied to,
　　　and the out-of-season rose
　　that turned into an epiphany: in
that uprush of forces, of faces, the anarchic
sweetness of it (it was twenty years
　　ago) I had my youth again.

Youth, in Tiananmen Square, arriving just
　　ahead of the great anniversary: was it
evidence of design in the weft of things,
　　that legion of messengers, headband-
wearers at once lighthearted and terrible,
　　as all angels are? O insomniac
　　　loveliness of arrival, of
　　exposure to the downpours of summer,
to the far, forgetful stars, those envoys
of long-undergone concussions, O insouciance
　　in the face of the forces of order.

Candlelight on the cobblestones of Leipzig;
　　in Prague a complicit candor, as night
after night we were drawn to the tube
　　(O brute honey, there in the dark,
though the smirk of mendacity contain it)
　　by the flowering, out in the snow, of so
　　　many faces: now that season's over.
　　But that freshet of anarchy,
while it lasted, halfway persuaded us
the archangels, whoever they are,
　　at moments are also human.

62

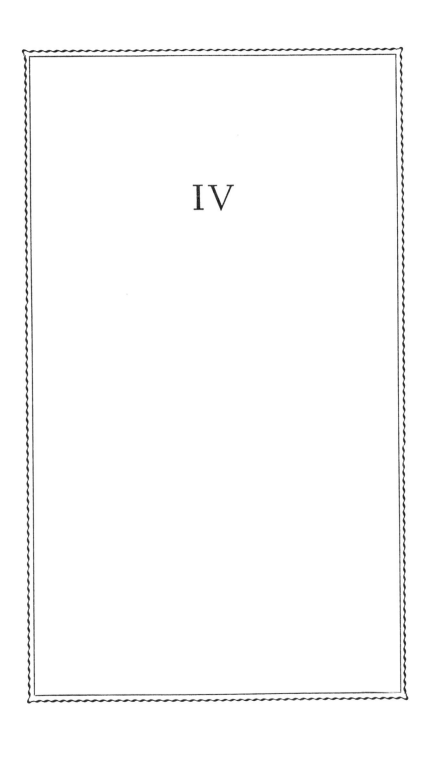

IV

AT MUKER,
UPPER SWALEDALE

To be wet was to be captive, idle and
poor. To be dry was to be free, indus-
trious and comfortable. This was the
lesson of the drowning cell.
— THE EMBARRASSMENT OF
RICHES, BY SIMON SCHAMA

The farmer with his milk pail
pausing, a fine rain falling,
burnishing with wet the wind-
nipped roof slates, fingering
the chimney-clumps of dwellings

following no plan or pattern
but that of having sat down,
one by one, as sheep would,
in the moor's high, wall-
ribbed, uncomfortable lee:

so it appears to one come as,
though country bred, a stranger,
to trudge the solitude of footpaths,
then early bed and, out of rural
sleep, dreams that are frantic

as Muker Beck aswirl, hurtling
to enter the River Swale: peat-
dark in spate, hour by hour
engorged with braidings, with
sheeted seethings of rainfall

fallen yet again: the trickle
of the damp's wrung increment
down limestone's fluted hollows
(buttertubs is what the locals
call them) that pock the pass

along the road to Askrigg—
slow, muted, single droplets
like bird notes after dark,
filterings ringleted with
brunet-stemmed spleenwort,

ageless as the lamb's cry,
the bees' noise, the lisp
of aeons. Strange, the lone
lapwing, the streamside fox-
glove, the harebell by the

roadside, the pale-eyed piebald
Swaledale breed, met up with
in one knockdown gathering,
the herdsman's yell (*Git in,
git in, git in, ye buggers*),

the neat small sheepdog doing
what it's bred for, all strange—
even the farmer's quasi-gentlemanly
tweed and Wellingtons: it's only
the milk pail takes me back to

the matriarchal smell of it,
warm from the udder; to manure-
pile, barnyard and stanchion,
green reek of silage, green
scum on the horse-trough,

year-round wall-sweat of old
farmhouses; to pump, sink,
cistern, slop pail for pigs,
the human slop jar, the gray
interminable hank of mildew.

Well, that's changing. Indoor
shivers give way (even here,
now that the heating's central)
to plush, florid wall-to-wall,
rippling fake fire, the daylong

warbling of the telly; to a
comfort wishfully aspired
toward, become no more than
the way we all—or if not all,
then most, or if not most,

the icons of our surrogate
existence—live now. Think,
though, of that roamer in the
rainy deserts of this shire,
the never-to-be-comfortable

George Fox, sworn enemy of
easy livings, of the steeple-
house's dry doldrums—who,
acquainted with the stink of
anybody in a state of nature,

a prisoner wading ankle-deep
in excrement, envisioning
beyond these elements a
heavenly rain descending,
aspired toward pure fire.

HOMELAND

Now and then the smell of apples
wrinkling in the dark wells up
from the earth-walled storm cellar

whose cold floor I last set foot on
so long ago, the wizened resins
of remembering turn into plunder.

To be homesick at all for what
we called the Cave: is it not rather
that we always had been strangers

to a habitat whose surface,
so recently still rippling
like a running weasel,

tree-darkened only in its stream-damp
secret parts, we'd bobbed, hairpinned
and pompadoured with farmsteads?

Windbreak and shelterbelt, the orchard
on its slope out past the feedlot:
against the weather's harnessless,

massive caprice, a corridor
of spruces to fend the blurred
thrust of it when, the last

Wolf River windfall gone to rot
in matted grass, the ciderpress
shut down, the crickets silent,

a shrieking solitude laid down
its curfew: to wring well-being
from indifference, to muster

shade and shelter from a realm
so bare of either: to put in
apple trees, to see them first

roseate, then whitening, then
bowed down with maroon, temptation's
emblem mellowing in the bin:

this was, one would have thought, the way
one came at last to feel at home.
One would have thought—were not

the Cave a witness, like the rod that,
climbing the siding, crowned the rooftree
with its finial, a glassblower's apple,

to unmitigated terror. We'd
been told that Jesus loved us,
but out there the old gods

slithered and swam uncaught,
and though we knew that no one
knew when one of them might next

flatten a crop or set a barn afire,
or worse, the bagged winds' black
archangel, even, had no proper name.

Had our forebears not put all but
plain talk behind them? Such
extravaganzas of suspense—

the brassy calm, the vapors' upthrust,
the lurid porches of foreboding
we lived among, they could be thought of

as a kind of homeland: the unease,
the dim notion of a down-to-earth
transcendence that brought us in,

that raises from the apple bin
long-dormant resonances
of an oncoming winter.

SED DE CORRER

Caught on the move—no knowing what year it was—
through the leaves of the ash tree outside the schoolroom,
the stumbling drone, the ineradicable blush, the botch
of being young: O how can I breathe, the eyes
are all mouths, they are drinking me—that glimpse:
a small bird, some part of it, among streakings
and shadings, the fluttering fan of it, afire
(a Blackburnian warbler? I ask myself now:
a redstart?) uncaught by the impeding
rigors of the vascular, the cambium's moist secrets
locked between xylem and phloem, the great, growing
trunk of it hardening, the mass, the circumference,
the unhurried, implacably already
there, that's to be escaped from:

escape, the urge to disjoin, the hunger
to have gone, to be going: *sed de correr:*
Vallejo in Paris writing (*me alejo todo*)
of fleeing, of running away from what made one,
from everything; Lorca, a stranger to
Morningside Heights, looking out from
that ridge above Harlem: the mire and fireflies,
the lit grid's apertures past counting,
the bleared eyeholes of jails: the tiered rictus
at Creedmore and Brentwood, where the mad
are warehoused, who do not look out of,
who burrow, denying the need for,
the nature and function, the very existence
of windows: holed up torpid, hibernal,
one day possibly (or possibly never),

fluttering, desiccated, frail,
to emerge from that hebetude:

the runaway halt, no opening other than
the starry apertures of paperwhite narcissus
forced in a bowl, cool, onion-rooted,
a sweetness I drank at as though entity
might depend from it: exploring
chlorinated caves of sensation (wet hair,
wool-steam, the pipes knocking), away from
the blare, out there, of certitude,
the glare of injunction: meaning
dwindling to a risen chain of bubbles
in the saucepan on the hotplate: the hurrying
fin far out, the lighthouse,
its pulsing aperture engulfed,
the waves breaking.

Virginia Woolf, having written her note of farewell,
going down to the river, the largest stone
she could manage shoved into her pocket: the body
of Lorca crumpling, shot down at the edge of
a pit on the outskirts of Granada: Vallejo
in Paris, in extremis, crying out on Good Friday
A.D. 1938, "I'm going to Spain!"—pulled up,
cut off from his own roots' torment,
the certitudes, the incursions, the plunder:
having written of the condition of cities,
of being alone among people: the windows looked out of,
the mute telephone, the dementia: Kafka
devising a passage up through the windowless
warren of calculation, contingency, foresight
there's no way out of, metamorphosing
escape in the form—O no, not of a bird,
not he who so fled the open, but of an insect

gravitating unerringly toward the dark:
those feelers, that lustrous, chitinous
lodging among interstices, among systems
we've lost track of the workings of,
and to whose advantage, outwitting
the gathering impasse of language, the screech
of its decibels, the mumble of its circumlocutions,
the mutter, all over Europe, of what sooner and sooner
was bound, was about to happen.

Refugees were arriving. Cut off, adrift, at large
in the fathomless afternoon of arrival,
alone—suppose that to be seen by no one
would be in fact to vanish?—I looked out from
a window ledge on Morningside Heights,
that ridge overlooking the eyesore
of real estate that is Harlem, too scared
to begin to grapple with, to think in
the inexorable terms of, the leverages
of excuse that maintained it: impervious
to the ideologue's whereases and necessarilys,
the thunderous because, the sad, lingering
cadenza of notwithstanding, I was not deaf to
the screech of what had somehow knowably—
how?—been closing in, closing down
ever since I'd begun to remember. Refugees:
it was with a refugee I'd venture,
just once, into Harlem: Jan Muller, who'd later,
vividly, paint his way through an insomniac
excess while he died of it, like Kafka. Refugees:
from the songless amputated tree
Lorca wrote of: leaves fallen, adrift,
the great trunk lost sight of, the stasis
of such scattering, such dispersals.

Adrift among hallways, stairwells, airshafts,
the asphalt of rooftops, among old-law walkups,
the rusting entablatures, fire escapes'
catfoot walkways, upended avenues of thievery,
of escape that is no escape: trailing the shuddering
jointed lurch alongside the platform, elevated
or submerged, the serial unseeing faces
within, the windows traveling, a delirium of them,
of arrivals, escapes that are no escape: cheap
plane tickets from Puerto Rico—to what? Rooftop
rainwater weeping in, the aerials, the hutches
put up by breeders of pigeons: the wild rock dove's
cosmopolitan offspring, their homing swerve
more nearly adapted than these refugees
from the canefields' corridored, murderous green,
caught up in the wingborne roar, the breaking
wave of displacement—so many injunctions
in need of translation—translated here, to
the crass miracle of whatever it is that put up
the South Bronx, street number after street number,
the mailbox pried open, recipient unknown,
moved on, shot down—and has made of it
this byword, this burnt-out, roofless, windowless
testimonial to systems gone rotten.
This arson.

There is much too much to be done: so Vallejo,
a wistful sometime disciple of Lenin,
declared: but who heard him? Not I,
shades drawn against being seen, against systems,
from bohemia's sempiternal cocoon, the hallways
smelling of cat piss and mildew. Who will hear?
Rilke wondered, imagining the rush from out there,
the vast presences, harsh with transcendence,
whose nature it is to ignore one. Not those great wings.

I was too much afraid. By a window
onto an airshaft one night I stood awed
at the sight of two men making love. I'd not
known how it was done. Through thin walls,
year after year, I could not stop up my ears to
the spats, the crudities, the climaxes
faked or unfaked, to (once) the squalled outcry
while others came to the rescue. What
my ears awaited, out past the suicidal refuge
of a fire escape on West Twelfth Street,
was the all-but-inaudible, the lisped *tsip*,
in a back-garden catalpa, the fluttering fan
of a warbler on the move: spring or fall,
that glimpsed inkling of things
beyond systems, windborne, oblivious.

Sed de correr: above Tijuana, where the language,
its streams and islets, begins to change color,
the moiling crawl along the freeway—
la cucaracha, the refuge of Gregor Samsa
writ large, written everywhere—a teenage
entrepreneur selling roses, bull's-blood-
red velvet of a piece with all the matador
kitsch across the border, threading the labyrinth
of the need to flee, to be at once on the go
and in hiding, that's what we've become.
The moving vehicle. The estrangement.
On West Twelfth Street, the tree is dying:
the rough, green-napped, huge heart shapes,
the cigar shapes, the striations at the throat
of the ruffled corolla, year by year, are
expiring by inches. The axe is laid
at the root of the ash tree. The leaves of dispersal,
the runaway pages, surround us. Who
will hear? Who will gather
them in? Who will read them?

A CADENZA

Puccini in hog-butchering time:
blood on the snow   the clockfaced
fearful valentine   DOCTOR IS IN
PLEASE BE SEATED   scarlatina
whooping cough   contagion
in the school gymnasium

Che gelida manina: "Your tiny
hand is frozen," the printed leaflet
idiotically rendered it. Everything
cultural somehow made people squirm.
Puck-seeny? It sounded like
some kind of figleaf: enough

to launch the ninth grade's darling
and her chum (who was plain), that evening,
onto high seas of silliness: "Your tiny . . ."
An aisle away, admiring and desolate,
I saw her as one whom privilege had bound for
the half-world of taffeta and gardenias,

Evening in Paris out of stoppered cobalt,
an apotheosis of merchandise,
la vie de bohème in a garret
become a commodity, along with,
as the houselights go down, malnutrition
and hypothermia, kept, needless to say,

at a tactfully discreet distance
away from the cold, the carcasses, blood
on the snow, the heartbeat thundering
inside the valentine—and the rampant
infection they had no name for. It
struck that same week, a peripeteia

leaving expectation moot. To hear of it,
whose blood did not run cold?
Mine does, still, at that giggling cadenza,
that conclusion dredged up from,
it must be, all of
six decades ago.

SEED

The way it came spinning onto the lawn—
the elm trees' chaffy currency, each piece
with a spot of seed at the center; the katydid-
colored, breeze-littering spindles let fall
by the maples; the squirm of catkins
fattening on the schoolyard poplars;
the way it annually left its smudge
like a bloodletting under the mulberry
in the first weeks of summer:

spring after spring, the same spangling,
smirching rain of it, making way
for yet other excesses—dewed,
swelling, softening to vegetable rot;
the fanged, maculate, pollen-triggering
tigerlily; the bearded rasp and
ripple of the barley; in field after
field, tasseled, seminal, knife-edged,
the green blades' rustle.

Nobody to hear the screams, if there
were any: . . . *found her* (a quasi-
prurient horror as the word went round) *down
in the cornfield. Strangled. And that ain't
all he* . . . Folks those days had trouble
saying it out loud. Some drifter. Never
caught. Whoever first set up the lingam
and called it Shiva—whatever minion of
some gross, overweening stud . . .

But wait. Remember, there was also Krishna,
flute-player, playboy, holding hands with
all the girls: the warm days glistening
with the feckless pollen of him, the nights
alive with yearning, the music of him,
the moist promises. And after? Doing
the reluctant decent thing. In haste,
stood up with by strangers. The neighbors
counting off the months.

Or that other, worse history, unhinted at
so long, appallingly unburdened one night
over a sepia portrait: *The one who died,
the prettiest of them: what really happened—
even in those days, in that family:
you knew?* Or the living issue, the tie
still unacknowledged: *God was cruel*—thus
Mrs. Transome to Denner, servant and
confidant—*when he made us women.*

And Denner: *I shouldn't like to be a man—
to cough so loud, and stand straddling about. . . .*
No matter. The moist, channeling silk awaits
the hanging tassel: *And in multiplying I
will multiply thy seed as the stars of heaven,
and as the sand which is upon the sea shore.* Or
as the storm of stuff the cottonwood squanders
in windrows on the sidewalk—even though
for a man to spend it thus

is, it is written, an abomination: as it is for
a woman to abort. See how the last mystery
rises to a travesty. Golf-cart sitcom.
The lingam huge, no joke. Steel-nippled
gorgon madonna of the primal scene.

I will make a song full of weapons, with
menacing points, and behind the weapons,
countless dissatisfied faces: thus
turbulent, fleshy, sensual,

eating and drinking and breeding Walt Whitman
(whom Emily Dickinson did not read, having
been told he was disgraceful),
celebrating the procreative urge, being himself
without issue: *of wombs and of the father-stuff,*
of sexes and lusts, voices veiled (he wrote),
and I remove the veil—which Edith Wharton
on the dreadful eve (she was twenty-three)
begged to have lifted

("You've looked at statues in museums, haven't you?"
her mother said, and coldly closed the subject):
who, childless, long schooled in discretion,
remembered sitting on the terrace at The Mount
late into the evening, hearing Henry James intone
the *Leaves of Grass*, extolling the father-stuff
above the lake, while fireflies signaled
the unending seedfall, the glinting
feculence of summer.

MATRIX
(Villa Serbelloni, Lake Como)

for Karen Chase

Perched for the nonce among such verticals,
such strata (And did the Principessa
have any friends down there?—O no,

she was *nobilità*), where history
is one long redoubt, where underlings
daily feed into the mangle, fold

on fold, the vellum-and-magnolia-petal
linens we sleep between—our dreams
burrow toward bedrock, down to the matrix,

as though the flinging open of so many
windows, such excess of light and air,
of attitude, the ease of bearing

up from the crypt, encysted, lapidary,
such indignities—the plucked eyeball
of Saint Lucy, Saint Roch's leprous thigh,

Sebastian, his lovely nakedness a grove,
a garden of undoing; the gouging
and the piercing, the vials held

by winged minions frantic lest a drop,
a berry from the tree of earthly horror
go unaccounted for; the ooze of blood,

O hideous, O precious—could not
but be requited by some warden of
the long-repressed, exhuming this

wrapped corpse: holy and dreadful,
the undisposed-of body of the mother.
Whose? The nightmare is not being sure.

Down by the lake we note, strolling a dense
memorial clutter, the dead baby, starkly
photographed; wreathed and embedded,

la moglie in mourning overhung
by the carved smirk of an upstart
lord and master; faceless in their nook

outside the walls, the name and birthplace
of the Englishman who drowned, whose fate
now furnishes the stony living-room

we who still live inhabit: outcrop and under-
croft, retaining wall where lizards hide,
the red valerian hangs, and busy daisies

here called *margheritas* burgeon in
a sun the cool spleenwort shrinks from;
precipice in whose still deeper shade

the violets of spring live on, as though
they'd undermine the summer; stone,
nurturer of Europe, the bereaved

exile's lost mother—otherwise
why this going back, these hankerings
after a relinquished privilege,

why her indentured hold on what we are
or could have been, why this unearned
nostalgia for the culture of the vine,

the pruning of the olive? Observing
how a laborer with a scythe, his
immemorial bending curve repeated

all afternoon, turned what had been a meadow
stippled first with buttercups, then the
beginning red of poppies, into a hayfield,

I thought (don't laugh) of Virgil
brooding on unrest in the metropolis,
knowing the countryside to be no idyl—

one's neighbors sly and fickle, played on
by superstitious rant. Some things
hardly change. There came an evening

toward the end of May, the cherries
reddening on the slope, when a small
procession, mainly of women, moved

up through the hayfield to a chapel
built in honor of My, Our, Their
Lady of the Monserrato, as every year

it had for, in this instance, precisely
the last four hundred. Some of us
came down (ah, feudal perquisites)

from dinner to look on. The Lady,
it appears, was Spanish to begin with,
named for a place denoting merely

a serrated peak. And so, above
her altar the Holy Child is shown
with, in his little hand, a little saw.

What *is* all this? Vigil candles
were fluttering; rosary-fingerers,
swaying as they sang, were singing

over and over, "Ave Maria, Madre di
Dio, tu sei la madre della Chiesa"—and
if, swaying with them, the pagan thrill

I felt had in it something wistful,
the thing I hankered after was no
rite but a foundation, the bedrock

that survives, the banded strata,
hurled reliquary of the drowned,
remnant of uncountable transformings:

precipice, gray limestone I've looked up
into the face of until the looking up
amounted to an attitude of worship:

stone that rings underfoot, whose surfaces
grow populous within doors as a tuned
instrument, eloquent of what lived once,

is now the stuff of cliffs, of crypts,
of hideaways. This morning, following
a track down to the lake, I came upon

a hollow in the cliff wall where,
drip-eroded, rosary-hung, dead flowers
littering the cave floor, there she was:

prayed to and put upon, another idol
of the universal mother. What *is*
all this? The infant in us still

won't let her go—lugubrious poppet,
nurturer, devourer: down below,
well-being's amniotic nightmare

still rocking to its own small music,
cradling the precipice—the clear,
uneasy, treacherous green water.

A SILENCE

past parentage or gender
beyond sung vocables
the slipped-between
the so infinitesimal
fault line
a limitless
interiority

beyond the woven
unicorn   the maiden
(man-carved   worm-eaten)
God at her hip
incipient
the untransfigured
cottontail
bluebell and primrose
growing wild   a strawberry
chagrin   night terrors
past the earthlit
unearthly masquerade

(we shall be changed)

a silence opens

☙

the larval feeder
naked   hairy   ravenous
inventing from within

itself its own
raw stuffs'
hooked silk-hung
relinquishment

behind the mask
the milkfat   shivering
sinew   isinglass
uncrumpling   transient
greed to reinvest

ﻬ

names have been
given   (revelation
kif   nirvana
syncope)   for
whatever gift
unasked
gives birth to

torrents
fixities
reincarnations of
the angels
Joseph Smith
enduring
martyrdom

a cavernous
compunction driving
founder-charlatans
who saw in it
the infinite

love of God
and had
(George Fox
was one)
great openings

NOTES

"SYRINX"
"Then there gathered from out of Erebus the spirits of those that are dead, brides, and unwedded youths, and toil-worn old men, and tender maidens with hearts yet new to sorrow, and many, too, that had been wounded with bronze-tipped spears, men slain in fight, wearing their blood-stained armour. These came thronging in crowds about the pit from every side, with a wondrous cry. . . ." —*Odyssey*, XI:34–43, translated by A. T. Murray (William Heinemann Ltd., 1919), vol. 1.

"DISCOVERY"
"Cape Canaveral, Fla., Jan. 22. Seven astronauts from three countries sailed flawlessly into orbit today aboard the space shuttle Discovery. . . ." —*The New York Times*, January 23, 1992.

"HISPANIOLA"
"Right from the start, Columbus had a plan: to establish a sugar industry on Hispaniola much like the ones back on the Canary and Madeira islands. . . ." —Susan Miller, "Slavery: The High Price of Sugar," *Newsweek*, Special Issue, Fall/Winter 1991.

"PAUMANOK"
> I too Paumanok, . . .
> I too leave little wrecks upon you, you fish-shaped island.
> —Walt Whitman, "As I Ebb'd with the Ocean of Life"

"MATOAKA"
The sources drawn upon here include *Their Majesties' Royall College: William and Mary in the Seventeenth and Eighteenth Centuries*, by J. E. Morpurgo (1976); *Narratives of Early Virginia*, edited by Lyon Gardner Tyler (1907); *Pocahontas*, by Grace Steele Woodward (1969); *The Virginia Guide* (1940, 1941); and *Undreamed Shores: England's Wasted Empire in America*, by Michael Foss (1974). The lines by Sir Walter

Raleigh are from "His Epitaph"; those by Michael Drayton, from "To the
Virginian Voyage."

"BROUGHT FROM BEYOND"
"Columbus's avidity for gold has been treated as a private obsession, but
[Jacques] Attali [in *1492*] claims that all Europe was in need of gold to
prevent trade 'asphyxiation.'" —Garry Wills, *The New York Review of
Books*, November 21, 1991.

"There was no talke, no hope, nor worke, but dig gold, wash gold, refine
gold, load gold. Such a brute of gold, as one mad fellow desired to be buried
in the sandes, least they should by their art make gold of his bones. . . ."
—*Narratives of Early Virginia*.

"What in part distinguished Sienese painting of the 15th century from
other Italian art was the liberal use of such expensive colors as gold and
ultramarine. . . . Intended to reflect the wealth and generosity of the
pictures' patrons, the use of such materials also had a specifically re-
ligious purpose, for by painting such opulent scenes, artists underscored
the distance between the viewer's life and the realm of the divine being
depicted. . . ." —Michael Kimmelman, "Sienese Gold," *New York Times
Magazine*, September 11, 1988.

"**bowerbird**, common name for any of several species of birds . . . native
to Australia and New Guinea, which build, for courtship display, a bower
of sticks or grasses. . . . Colored stones, shells, feathers, flowers, and other
bright objects . . . are used. . . . The satin bowerbird, *Ptilonorhyncus
violaceus*, prefers blue decorative articles." —*The Columbia Encyclopedia*

"THE UNDERWORLD OF DANTE"
This canto of the *Inferno* finds Dante with his guide, the Roman poet
Virgil, halted beside the River Styx, which forms a moat about the city of
Dis (the "doleful metropolis"), the stronghold of Satan and his rebel angels.
The Furies or Erinyes, the Gorgon Medusa—one look at whom was said to
turn the viewer to stone—the watchdog Cerberus, and the heroic figure of
Theseus are all drawn from classical mythology.

"SHOREBIRD-WATCHING"
The Althing is the parliament of Iceland. "Thingstead" is the name given
to the meeting place of such a body.

"THINKING RED"
The interview with the physicist George Wald referred to here was reported by Estelle Gilson in *Columbia Magazine*, October 1985.

"THE WAR MEMORIAL"
George Fox (1624–91), the English reformer who founded the Society of Friends, reported in his *Journal* the incident referred to here.

" 'EIGHTY-NINE"
> . . . Not that you could bear
> the voice of God—far from it. But hear the wind's blowing,
> the uninterrupted tidings created from silence,
> they sweep toward you now from those who died young.
> . . .
> Every angel is terrible. And yet, alas,
> I welcome you, almost fatal birds of the soul. . . .
>   —Rainer Maria Rilke, *Duino Elegies*,
>   translated by C. F. MacIntyre

"SED DE CORRER"
The Complete Posthumous Poetry of Cesar Vallejo, translated by Clayton Eshleman and José Rubía Barcia (1978), is the source of the passages quoted here. *Poet in New York*, by Federico García Lorca, translated by Greg Simon and Steven F. White (1988), has been similarly drawn upon. I am indebted to Cecilia Vicuña for particular help and inspiration.

"SEED"
The characters of Mrs. Transome and her maid Denner appear in George Eliot's novel *Felix Holt*. The lines by Whitman are from his "Song of Myself." Edith Wharton's memoir, *A Backward Glance*, records the presence of Henry James at The Mount, her home in the Berkshires; an unfinished account entitled "Life and I" (in *Novellas and Other Writings*, Library of America) tells of the incident before her marriage.

"MATRIX"
"The Madonna of Montserrato is one of the most revered Madonnas of Spain, before whose statue in the abbey of Montserrato St. Ignatius Loyola laid down his sword and dagger to become a warrior of the church. . . . The

oil painting of the Madonna that graces the present 19th-century chapel, by style clearly of the late 16th century and hence an altar piece in the original church [built at Bellagio by Ercole Sfondrati in the year 1591], portrays a Madonna holding the Child . . . wielding a saw like those still seen in Bellagio, a small 'buck-saw,' and he is using it to cut saw teeth into the mountains in the background. Perhaps the implication is that the Child sawed off the great slab of limestone on which the Bellagio chapel stands. Have we here a kind of baroque pun? It is a fact that in the Spanish Montserrato there is a dim tradition that its saw-toothed mountains were shaped by angels wielding golden saws."　—*The Castle's Keep: The Villa Serbelloni in History*, by John Marshall (1970), p. 101.

"A SILENCE"

". . . while walking one day in Boston, he saw the streets suddenly shrink and divide. His everyday preoccupations, his past, all the claims of the future fell away and he was enfolded in a great silence. . . . At the age of twenty-one [T. S.] Eliot had one of those experiences which, he said, many have had once or twice in their lives and been unable to put into words." —*Eliot's Early Years*, by Lyndall Gordon (1977), p. 15.

". . . dignity and majesty have I seen but once, as it stood in chains at midnight in a dungeon in an obscure village in Missouri."　—Letter written by Parley Pratt on Joseph Smith in jail, quoted by Fawn Brodie in *No Man Knows My History: The Life of Joseph Smith* (1986), p. 243.

". . . also I saw the infinite love of God, and I had great openings." —*The Journal of George Fox.*

ACKNOWLEDGMENTS

Some of the poems in this collection originally appeared in the following publications:

Antaeus: "From the Underworld of Dante: Canto IX"

New England Review / Bread Loaf Quarterly: "Eighty-Nine"

The New Republic: "Birdham," "The Horned Rampion"

The New Yorker: "At Muker, Upper Swaledale," "Brought from Beyond," "A Cadenza," "Discovery," "In Umbria: A Snapshot," "Paumanok" under the title "North Fork"

Nimrod: "Green"

The Paris Review: "Matrix," "Seed"

Partisan Review: "Shorebird-Watching" under the title "Shorebirds in Seasonal Plumage Observed Through Binoculars"

Poetry Review (London): "Syrinx"

Puckerbrush Review: "At Easterly"

Shenandoah: "Manhattan"

Southwest Review: "Homeland"

stet (Dublin): "White"

Verse: "Hispaniola," "Thinking Red"

The William and Mary Review: "Nondescript"

The Yale Review: "Sed de Correr"

Canto IX of the *Inferno* of Dante, as reprinted here, is part of *Dante's Inferno: Translations by Twenty Contemporary Poets*, edited by Daniel Halpern (Ecco Press, 1993).

"Bayou Afternoon" first appeared in *Everything Comes to Light: A Festschrift for Joy Scantlebury*, edited by Leo Luke Marcello (The Cramers Press, 1993).

"Matoaka" was originally published as a pamphlet by the College of William and Mary, Willliamsburg, Virginia, in February 1993. It has been reprinted in *Verse* and elsewhere.

"The War Memorial" first appeared in *After the Storm*, edited by Jay Meek and F. D. Reeve (Maisonneuve Press, 1992).

"Manhattan" was reprinted in a limited edition entitled *Manhattan: An Elegy and Other Poems* (The University of Iowa Center for the Book, 1990).

"Green," "Paumanok" (as "North Fork"), "Seed," and "Shorebird-Watching" (as "Shorebirds in Seasonal Plumage Observed Through Binoculars") were reprinted in *Poems for a Small Planet: Contemporary American Nature Poetry*, edited by Robert Pack and Jay Parini (Middlebury College Press, 1993).

Grateful acknowledgment is made to the University of California Press for permission to reprint four lines from "The First Elegy" and two lines from "The Second Elegy" from Rainer Maria Rilke, *Duino Elegies*, translated and edited by C. F. MacIntyre, copyright © 1961 by C. F. MacIntyre.

The author is further indebted to the Lila Wallace–Readers Digest Foundation, to the John D. and Catherine T. MacArthur Foundation, and to the Bellagio Study and Conference Center of the Rockefeller Foundation for their support.

Amy Clampitt was born and brought up in New Providence, Iowa, graduated from Grinnell College, and has since lived mainly in New York City. Her first full-length collection, *The Kingfisher*, published in 1983, was followed in 1985 by *What the Light Was Like*, in 1987 by *Archaic Figure*, and in 1990 by *Westward*. The recipient in 1982 of a Guggenheim Fellowship, and in 1984 of the fellowship award of the Academy of American Poets, she was made a MacArthur Prize Fellow in 1992. She is a member of the American Academy of Arts and Letters and has been Writer in Residence at the College of William and Mary, Visiting Writer at Amherst College, and Grace Hazard Conkling Visiting Writer at Smith College.

A NOTE ON THE TYPE

This book was set in Fairfield, the first typeface from the hand of the distinguished American artist and engraver Rudolph Ruzicka (1883–1978). In its structure Fairfield displays the sober and sane qualities of the master craftsman whose talent was dedicated to clarity. It is this trait that accounts for the trim grace and virility, the spirited design and sensitive balance, of this original typeface.

Rudolph Ruzicka was born in Bohemia and came to America in 1894. He designed and illustrated many books, and was the creator of a considerable list of individual prints—wood engravings, line engravings on copper, and aquatints.

Composed and printed by Heritage Printers,
Charlotte, North Carolina
Bound by Kingsport Press, Kingsport, Tennessee
Designed by Peter A. Andersen